The Wonderful Life of Russia's Saint Sergius of Radonezh

Told by Alvin Alexsi Currier

•

Illustrated by Nadezda Glazunova

Conciliar Press
Ben Lomond, California

Published by Conciliar Press
P.O. Box 76, Ben Lomond, California 95005

Printed in Hong Kong

Book Design & Typography by Arthur Durkee

Library of Congress Cataloging-in-Publication Data

Currier, Alvin Alexsi.
    The wonderful life of Russia's Saint Sergius of Radonezh / told by
Alvin Alexsi Currier; illustrated by Nadezda Glazunova.
    p.   cm.
    ISBN 1–888212–24–1
    1. Sergii, Radonezhskii, Saint, ca. 1314–1391 or 2.–Juvenile
literature.
    2. Christian saints–Russia–Biography–Juvenile literature.
    [1. Sergius, of Radonezh, Saint, ca. 1314–1391 or 2. 2. Saints.]

    I. Glazunova, Nadja, ill.   II. Title.
BX597.S45 C87   2001
281.9'092–dc21   2001028690

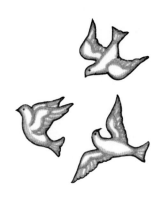

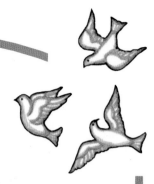

When Saint Sergius was a little boy, his name was Bartholomew.

He loved the forest.

He could stand for hours and watch the birds soar or watch the bugs crawl. Ever since he was old enough his father had sent him to tend the horses in the woods.

He loved the forest almost as much as he loved his mother and father. He loved his brothers Stephen and Peter. He loved God. He loved going with his family to the rich services and celebrations of the beautiful Churches and monasteries of the city of Rostov where he lived. He wanted to become a monk and move into the forest and be forever with God in prayer. He loved God. He loved his family. He loved the Church, and he loved the vast forests of God's creation. He loved everything, everything except school. No matter how hard he tried he couldn't learn to read and write.

His classmates easily learned to turn letters into sounds, words, sentences, and meaning; but for Bartholomew these same letters only turned into birds that flew off with him to circle in the blue sky above the forest, or the letters would change into little bugs that crawled off with him into the woodland undergrowth. It hurt so much that he couldn't learn to read or write. His parents were displeased, his classmates teased, and the headmaster continued to scold him.

So on the day when our story begins we find him as a seven year old boy, wandering in the forest, sad, sorry, and hurting.

On this special day
His father had sent him away
To find a foal in the forest,
But instead of the foal he found a sight
That filled him with awe and wonder.
Under an oak tree up ahead
An aged monk stood praying.
Silently the boy drew near
And watched and watched and waited.
At the end of his prayers
The monk looked to the boy
And asked what he wanted and needed.
Bartholomew poured out his pain and his fright
Because he could not learn to read or write.
The withered old monk raised his hands in prayer
Then lowered them to a bag that hung at his waist
And from that bag he withdrew a piece
Of the holy, blessed bread that he carried.
"This bread is a sign," he softly said,
"That now by God's grace
You can read and write,
As well or even better than others."
There they talked, this monk and the boy
Until the shadows announced the coming of night
And the boy begged the monk to come to his home
For evening prayers and a supper.
Bartholomew's parents welcomed with joy
The stranger their son had brought them,
But when the monk gave the boy a book
And asked him to read evening prayers,
The boy did plead: "I cannot read,"
But the monk only said,
"Remember the bread,"
And then, indeed, Bartholomew saw he could read,
And he read, and read, and read.

Soon times turned bad within the walls
Of the rich old city of Rostov
And his parents, his brothers, and Bartholomew
Gathered together what little they could
Of their household and goods
And fled south to a town called Radonezh.
In Radonezh by the Church of Christ's Birth
The family found peace
And both of his brothers were married.
But Bartholomew asked of his father instead
His leave to go live as a monk in the forest.
"My son," said his father, "please wait a little,
For both of your brothers have families to feed
And we are old and weak and have a need
Of someone to tend and to care for us."
In just a few years these parents passed on
And by their sons they were buried.
For forty days their sons watched by their graves,
Then Bartholomew sold all that he had
And gave his inheritance to Peter his brother.
Brother Stephen already had lost his wife
And given his life to live as a monk in God's service.
Now begged by his brother to join him,
Stephen left behind the monastic walls,
And together the two
Plunged into the forest's vast darkness,
Searching far and searching near
Until at last they found a hill
Beside a stream, and knew it was here
That they were meant to build their cell and their chapel.

So it was that over seven hundred years ago the young
man Bartholomew and his brother the monk Stephen
raised a cross in the dark forested wilderness and
founded their hermitage dedicated to the Holy Trinity.

Once the cross was raised at the place they had found
The brothers hurriedly turned around
And headed back out of the woods
Past the farms, settlements, and towns
To the city of Moscow at the heart of the land
To seek a blessing from the Metropolitan's hand
To build a Church on the site they had found.
Receiving the blessing they returned to their woods
And before it snowed there was a cell to live in
And before it snowed again there was a Church to pray in
And before it snowed for the third winter
Stephen left for his old monastic home
And Bartholomew at last was all alone,
Alone with God his creator
And all of God's creatures
Deep in the dark Russian forest
Deep in God's cathedral of creation.
His holy prayers like a shimmer of grace
Swiftly flowed out of the chapel to encircle the space
As all creation found its place
In a harmony of worship.
Even a bear became quiet and tame
And again and again for a year he came
And Bartholomew shared his bread with this brother.
In the third year of his life as a hermit
The Abbot Metrophanes came to his forest to pray
And Bartholomew bowed before him to say:
"My Father, show charity to me
And grant me to enter the monastic state,
For I have desired it from my youth,
Only the pleas of my parents held me back,
But now I am free and I thirst for living water."
So on that very day, the seventh of October
In the year of thirteen hundred and thirty-seven
Bartholomew was tonsured a monk
And given the holy name of Sergius.

Finally in the forest
In relation to creation
The spiritual life of Sergius
Found its fulfillment
In the harmony
Of the trinity
Of Creature, Creator, and Creation.
Round and round through days and seasons
Through praying working, working praying
A holy light started glowing
A spiritual radiance started growing
And following it like a star
Pilgrims came from near and far.

How long Sergius lived alone
Is not really known
But what is clear
Is that there did soon appear
A whole little village of men singing prayers
And all the legends tell
How Sergius helped each to build his cell.
And so they lived for many years
Until there came the Patriarch's urging
That it was not right to live alone
With many things that were one's own
But rather everything they should share
Each with all and all with each
Their life, their labor, and their prayer.
And so was born the family
Of the Holy Trinity Monastery
And in this unity of community
Holy Sergius chose his place
Seeking out the lowest task
Whether sowing seeds or hoeing weeds
As the least and humblest servant of all.

To the evil one of this earth
The sweet incense of prayer
Became an abominable stench
And the devil soon sought every means known to his craft
To steal through the protecting walls of prayer
And enter into the hearts of the holy monks
To seek some leftover coals of the human fires
Of doubt and fear, greed and envy
And finding here and there a smoldering coal
The devil called all his legions
To fan it into flame again
Until the fires of discontent flamed up in the monastery.
Sergius saw at once the devil's hand in the fires of
        bickering and doubt among the monks
And he summoned them to arm themselves with the
Weapons of faithfulness and prayer.
So the long age of holy warfare with the forces of evil
Settled over the monastery
And from it the age of signs and wonders dawned.

In one attack the evil one caused the supplies of food to
dwindle until the monastery kitchen had nothing left
to prepare for a meal.
Hunger began to burn in the bellies of the monks
And they came to Sergius to plead that they should go into
the village to buy, beg, or borrow some food.
The Saint called them to continue to trust God
And he shared his share of the few crumbs that they found
to eat with others.
The sun continued to rise, to set, and to return again
And the raging fires of hunger began to roar with the
devil's mockery of their trust in God.
Barely but just barely Sergius held them together
With his holy trust and faith
Until one evening in their weakness
They heard the creaking of a cart coming up the road,
And to their amazement a horse-drawn wagon appeared
Heavy laden with food
The fresh bread still warm from the oven
And the drivers of the cart explained
That a wealthy merchant in the city
Had sent the wagon full of food
As an offering of love for the faithfulness
Of the monks and the monastery
And all of them together raised their eyes to heaven
And gave thanks to God for this miracle
Of God's answer to their prayers
And the devil slithered away in defeat.

Now once upon another time
As the number of monks grew
The devil encouraged them to haul the water freely
From the little stream that served the monastery.
This they did until the creek became shallow
And their hauling muddied the waters.
The monastery began to lack clean water to drink
And water to wash and to work with.
The devil delighted in the desperate plight
But Sergius never lost sight
Of God's promise to guide and protect him.
Alone with his friend he left the hill
Of the monastic Church and its buildings
And seeking the forest not far away
He sought out a lonely place to pray
A place that deep in the dark of the woods did lay.
And there while he knelt so deep in prayer
Slowly he became aware
That the ground grew moist beneath him.
Water bubbled up from under the grass
And there a miracle came to pass
As a crystal clear stream started flowing.
And to this day if you pass this way
You can still see this spring of St. Sergius
Where in summer's heat and winter's snow
The faithful still come to bathe in the flow
And fill their containers with water
For here they know
God did show
A miracle
And the devil's defeat
In response to the prayer of St. Sergius.

Yet again on another occasion
A poor devout peasant was plunged into grief
As his son took ill
Growing weaker and weaker every day
Until at last death had its way
And the boy died in the arms of his father.
The peasant lived close to the monastery's wall
And as the news of the death was heard
Holy Sergius felt a call
So he left his work and made his way
To the peasant's hut where the dead boy lay.
Beside the body, the Saint knelt down
And made his prayer, kneeling there
Until a miracle started occurring
As in the lifeless form there came a stirring
And slowly his breath returned to breathing
And his body warmed to life.

Inconsolably lamenting the father returned to his hut
In his arms carrying
A coffin for his son's burying.
Only slowly, slowly did he grasp what he did see
His son from the bonds of death was free
And weeping the father fell to his knee
Praising God with tears of joy
For giving him back his little boy.

Outwardly for all to see
Many miracles came to be
But to Sergius alone
Inwardly and out of sight
At the altar or in the night
Came wonders wrapped in a mystical light
Or blazing in a brilliance bright
Leaving only his soul with eyes to see
These visions with which God blessed him.
One stormy dark night while deep in prayer
Fervently for his monks praying
Somewhere outside where the wind was blowing
Amid the trees swaying
A voice was crying, a whisper was saying:
"Sergius, Sergius."
So praying a prayer to calm his fright
He opened the door and went out to the night.
There from heaven there shone such a light
That all the forest was glowing and bright
And through the wind a voice was heard,
"Sergius, Sergius, hear this word,
Your prayer has been heard,
Your prayer for your disciples.
Now Sergius, Sergius look and see
The multitude of monks
Gathered together into your fold
The fold of the Holy Trinity."
And raising his eyes to the light in the night
Radiant birds in swirling flocks flew into his sight
Singing the angelic hymn in unspeakable sweetness.
Again on the wind the voice was heard:
"Your disciples shall number not less than these birds,
And if in your footsteps they follow
Like the winged creatures of heaven they shall sing
And be adorned with every virtue."

In all reports the truth is told
That Sergius remained quiet and humble.
So it was that it once came to pass
That a rich merchant came seeking the elder.
The monks pointed Sergius out, but alas
The merchant thought they were joking.
For all he saw was a monk stooped and old
Hoeing the garden out in the cold
In a cassock torn and tattered.
Later that day when a Prince arrived in his royal gown
It was before that old monk that he did bow down
And as the crowd gathered around the two
The merchant knew who was who
And realized his folly.

Ah, but in another place
In a very holy space,
Isaac and Macarius
Two monks of virtue and full of grace
Were granted a most amazing sight
As Sergius served at the altar.
Behind the Saint they clearly saw
As they stood in holy awe
An angel also serving.
And Simon the monk saw a similar sight
As Sergius at the altar served
Around him swirled a fire of light
Holy flames flashing bright
Twirling down in swirling blazing
Into the chalice he was raising.

The Saint acknowledged what the monks had observed
That heavenly hosts always with him served
But humbly he said,
"Tell no one of this until I am dead."

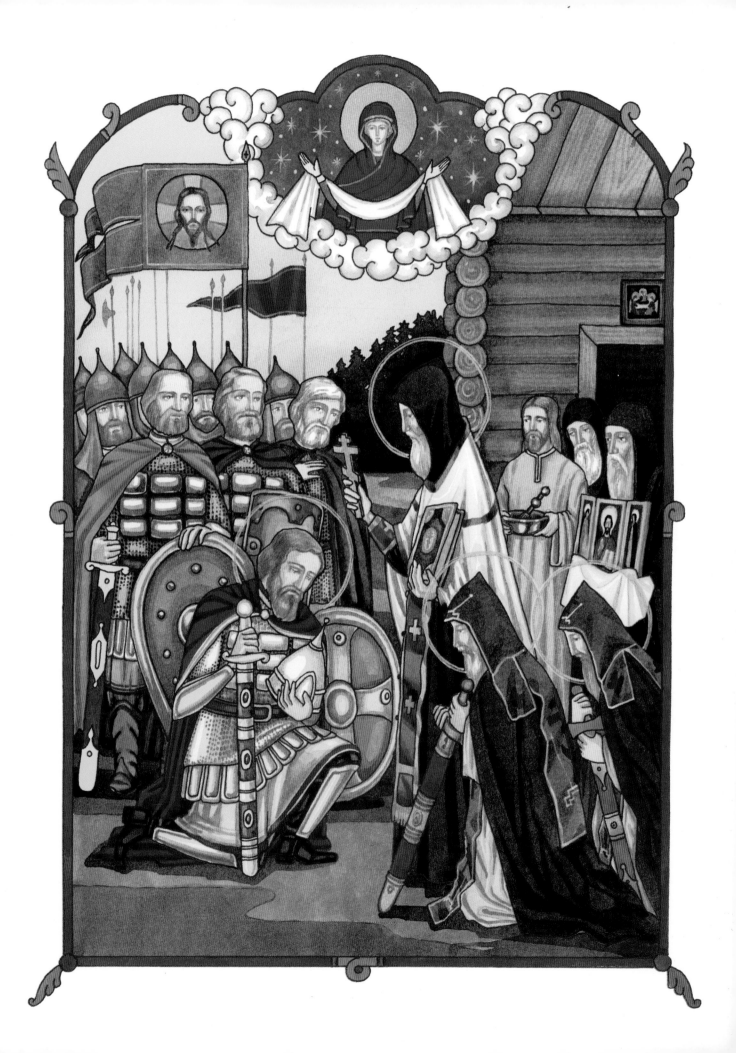

Then suddenly
Into the world of holy prayer
Orbiting through the circling year
News of the Tartar horde was heard
News of ruthless rage that seized the heart with fear
Galloping, galloping ever more near
Like evil waves washing across Russia.
They burned cities, murdered their inhabitants,
And laid heavy taxes on the nation.
It was the year of our Lord thirteen hundred and eighty.

Grand Prince Dimitri tried as best he could
To rally the bickering Russian rulers
But he saw with fear as the hordes drew near
That his army was sorely outnumbered.
So with his military leaders and the few loyal princes
To Holy Trinity Monastery he journeyed forth
To ask St. Sergius the abbot what he should do.
First the abbot inquired if the Grand Prince had explored
All avenues to peace and alternatives to war
And the Prince replied that all had been tried
And there was nothing more
That he could see to say or do.
Then it was that St. Sergius held in his hand
The fate of the mighty Russian land.
Then he blessed Prince Dimitri to go forth into battle,
Predicting that bloody would be the cost
But the cause in the end would not be lost.
And when came the day, though it was far away
With clairvoyant sight, he saw every stroke of the fight
As with all of his monks he stood praying.
And from the morning's first light on into the night
He named every man who fell dying.
Finally from the altar he turned to his monks
And announced to all that the battle was done
And Russia had won.

So the years passed in the life of the Saint
And there many other tales as well
That if we had time, we could tell
But we dare not end, without the story
Of the Holy Saint's final and greatest glory.

One night in his cell
After praying his usual rule of prayer
And special hymns to God's Mother as well
He sat down to rest in a chair.
And from his quiet while sitting there
To his disciple Micah he whispered: "Beware,
Be calm and be bold,
For a wondrous vision we're about to behold."
Instantly a voice was heard,
"Lo, the Blessed Virgin comes."
Hearing this the Saint rushed forth from his cell
To the corridor radiant with dazzling light.
Where the Mother of God met his sight
Together with the Apostles Peter and John.
There Sergius fell to the ground
With the bright white light all around
As the Mother of God reached out to touch him
While speaking this word:
"Have no fear, for your prayers have been heard,
Henceforth through the ages this monastery will flourish
For it, I myself shall protect and shall nourish."
Having thus spoken, she vanished.

rembling there in wonder and awe
The Saint slowly rose up and suddenly saw
His disciple as one dead on the ground.
He gently roused the terror-struck man.
The disciple swiftly fell at his elder's feet
And pleadingly asked the meaning of what he had seen.
But so stunned was Sergius by the resplendent vision
That he simply asked his disciple to wait
While he calmed down from his ecstatic state.
Finally for Simon and Isaac he sent
And after telling them all, together they all went
To sing a service of Thanksgiving
And through the rest of the night
With his face bathed in light
The Saint meditated on his visit.

Today more than six hundred years
Have fallen like leaves from the tree of time
Since that day long ago when St. Sergius
Fell asleep in the Lord.
But like a carpet of leaves,
His life and deeds
Color and cover the course of history.
Into the forests his disciples plunged
Founding across the Russian lands
Over fifty communities before he died
And forty in the next generation.
And over the centuries
The Monastery of the Holy Trinity grew
Until today, with golden domes against the sky of blue
Still protected by the Holy Mother
It is the spiritual heart of Russia.
And with still wider circles around the globe
The whole of the Orthodox world sings:

"Champion of virtue and warrior of Christ,
thou didst contend against earthly passions;
thou wast a model to thy disciples in vigil,
chant and fasting
and the Holy Spirit came and dwelt in thee.
As thou hast boldness towards the Trinity
remember thy flock
and visit thy children as thou didst promise,
O holy Father Sergius."

Troparion of St. Sergius in the fourth tone.
The feast day of St. Sergius is celebrated
on September 25, which is October 8
on the old calendar.

About the Illustrator

Nadezda Glazunova began her artistic career in her native Russia by painting in a communist souvenir factory. Her obvious talent won her admission to the National College of Traditional and Folk Art, where she met her husband, Leonid, a master woodcarver. After graduation and marriage they made their home in Petrozavodsk, working together as artists. In 1990, with the fall of communism, Nadezda received her first commission. It was to create religious Christmas and Easter cards. In 1991 those first cards were printed in Vienna, Austria, and since then her many cards have had a continuous market in Europe and America.

Working with author Alvin Alexsi Currier, she illustrated her first book, *The Miraculous Child*, which was published in German and English in Vienna in 1995. A second book from this team, *Alyosha's Apple*, was published in 1999.

Nadezda's work, full of color, life, and joy, reflects her longing for her beloved country to return to the kind of life, rooted in the faith and traditions of Orthodoxy, that she depicts in her paintings. Today she lives with her husband and son in a modest old wooden home near to the golden-domed monastery of the Holy Trinity in Sergiyev Posad, in Russia.

About the Author

Outwardly Alvin Alexsi Currier is known as a son of the city of Minneapolis, and until his retirement after 35 years, he was classified professionally as a Presbyterian clergyman who served various midwestern American churches, two parishes in Germany, and for eleven years as a college chaplain.

Inwardly he is a pilgrim who, sensing his spiritual emptiness, fled professional life for the forest in 1975. There in the following two decades he lived a semi-monastic life, founding and tending St. Herman's Hermitage as a place of prayer for all people, and finding his spiritual home in the Orthodox Church.

Today with his wife Anastasia he lives in St. Paul, Minnesota, as an author, artist, and interpreter of Orthodoxy, traveling widely in Eastern Europe and organizing pilgrimages of mutual encouragement for others to experience Orthodoxy from the inside out. His other books include: *Karelia: An Introduction to, and Meditation on, Karelian Orthodox Culture, Alyosha's Apple, The Miraculous Child,* and *How the Monastery Came to Be on Top of the Mountain.*